Knights

Suzan Boshouwers & Marjolein Hund

Clavis
NEW YORK

Harry, Ken and Hanna are playing knights
and maidens. Harry and Ken are the knights
and Hanna is the maiden.
Look, they built a castle with towers, a flag
and a big gate.

The knights are going on a journey today.
Watch out! It's dangerous outside the gates.
They have to be careful of wild animals
and raiders. Luckily, knights are never afraid.
Have a good trip, brave knights!
All of a sudden...

This is where I live

A knight lives in a castle, but the castle doesn't belong to him.
It belongs to the king.
In exchange, the knight protects all the people that live nearby.
So a knight works for the king.
It's a big honor!

It's exciting to live in a castle. There are many rooms
and towers, and long hallways.
The thick walls and the high towers
protect the people who live in it during
times of war or when raiders attack.
Can you see the castle where I live?

Did you know
the word knight
comes from West Germanic
words meaning "servant"?

This is what a knight does

A knight has to protect the castle
and all the people living nearby. He is somewhat of a soldier.
Fighting, being brave, helping sick and poor people, being a hero,
making long journeys, hunting — a knight does all those things.

My knight doesn't wear a soldier's uniform, he wears a suit of
armor. A suit of armor is an outfit made out of steel.
It protects the knight's entire body when he has to fight.
The suit of armor is very heavy, so it's difficult to put on.
The shield-bearer helps the knight to do that.

Did you know
shield-bearers often
play games wearing
parts of the suit of armor?
That way they get used
to moving around in such
heavy clothes.

Did you know
horses and other
animals sometimes
wear armor too?

This is what I do

One day I will be a knight! That's not easy. You have to be from a family of knights and you have to practice a lot. Because I worked really hard, I was given the important job of shield-bearer. I am always ready to help my knight. At home, I have to do lots of things.

practice swordsmanship

learn how to fight
with a lance

polish helmets
until they shine

learn how to ride horseback

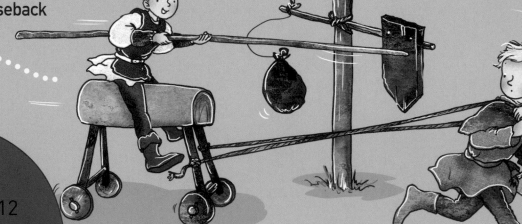

Did you know

a lance can be up to 12 feet long? Try taking four giant steps. That's about 12 feet.

Did you know some knights give their swords a name? The famous king Arthur called his magical weapon "Excalibur". If you had a sword, what would you call it?

I learn to do other things as well, like shooting with a crossbow, singing, reading and writing, searching for wood for the hearth-fire....
My sister Hanna does none of those things.
Girls usually stay in the castle.
Their mothers teach them how to spin and weave and they learn how to keep the castle running.

Did you know a shield-bearer gets his own sword and his own shield when he becomes a knight? He also gets to pick his own shield-bearer.

This is how you become a knight

A shield-bearer has to practice and work for ten years.
Only then can he become a knight. When the big day arrives
the shield-bearer puts on a beautiful red coat and
goes to visit the king. There's a big party: flags fly everywhere
and there are trumpets playing. When it's time for the ceremony,
the shield-bearer kneels before the king and promises that
he will always be honest and hard-working. Then the king
softly taps the shield-bearer's shoulder with his sword.
That's the signal that the shield-bearer has become a knight!

horse for the knight

protection
for the horse

breast plate

sword

leg protector

shield

shield-bearers

helmet

gloves

farrier

servant girls

jester

maiden

knight

This is how we celebrate!

When the sun sets, the people go to a big party in the castle.
There is a lot to eat and drink. Big tables hold vegetables,
meat, game, soup, fish, and fruit. There is plenty for everyone.
Look, there is even a decorated swan!
The knight who won the tournament has a place of honor.
He gets to sit at the biggest table!

Did you know
at some parties,
there are performances
by dancing bears?

jester

Did you know
we use our hands to eat?
It's not rude, we always do that!

Jugglers and musicians provide entertainment during the meal. There is a minstrel. That's someone who sings songs and plays music. He also tells stories and brings the latest news about tournaments for knights! Of course, the jester is also here!

minstrel

This is how I say goodbye

After dinner, the tables get pushed aside and we start dancing. The minstrel plays music.
The party isn't over until much later, when almost everybody falls asleep.

This was my story about my life as a shield-bearer and about the life of knights.
I hope you had a good time in the castle and at this party.

Now, it's time to sing my final song.

In the evening hour
we come together in the tower.
And after the knights have eaten well,
they listen to the story I tell.
About swords, and horses and
very brave knights,
going to tournaments and
practicing fights.
About shield-bearers outside and
maidens indoors,
working hard and doing their chores.
And when my story ends,
I say goodbye to all my friends!

Goodbye!

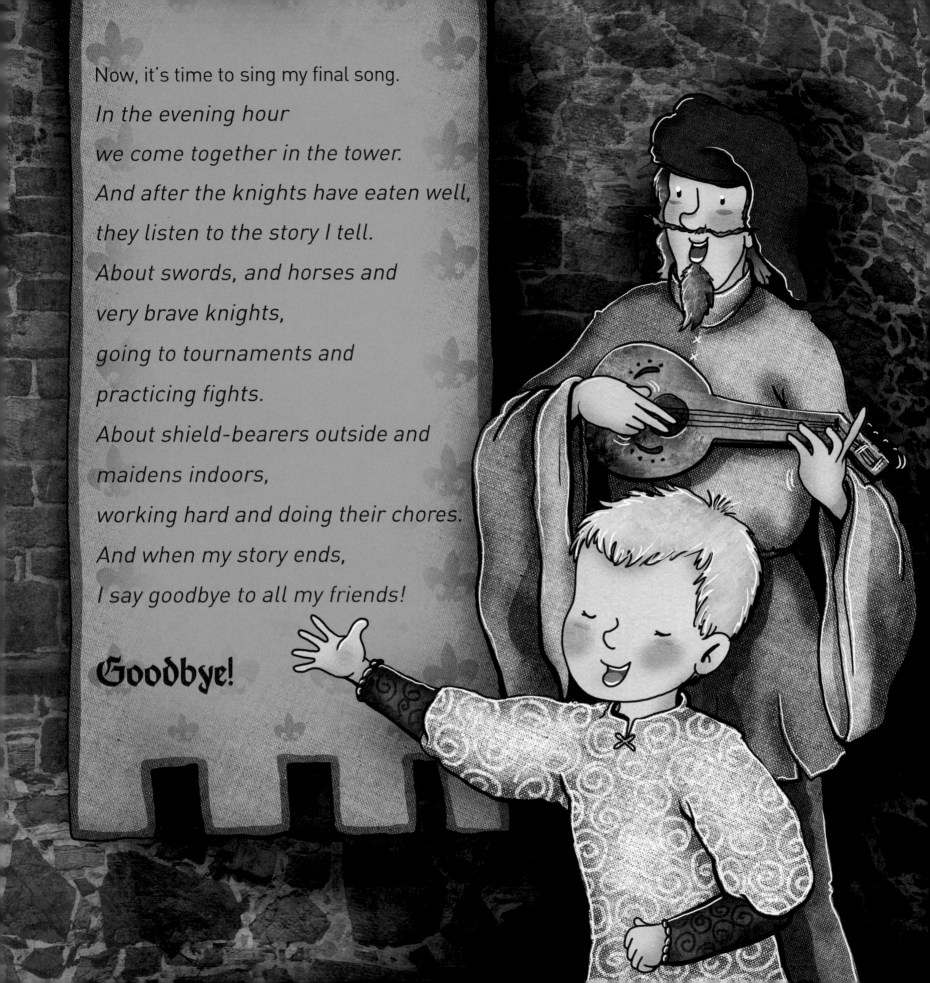

These are famous knights

Many great stories have been written about knights.
There are stories about brave knights who are never afraid.
And stories about knights who fought dragons and witches!
But many of those knights never really existed.
The stories are simply made up!

The most famous knight of all is **Arthur**. He came from England. He had a big Round Table, with room for twelve knights. They were a real club, and they called themselves "**The Knights of the Round Table**". But nobody knows for sure if Arthur and his club ever really existed.

The story of **George** and the Dragon is very famous. George wasn't a knight, but a shield-bearer. He carried an old shield made of silver, with a big red cross on it. George defeated a dragon that was so big and dangerous that no one else could. George has become a real hero.

Don Quixote is the main character in a book. He thinks he is a brave knight, but he really isn't. He just imagines he is. He fights windmills because he thinks they are giants! And he has many funny adventures like that.

Did you know
when no one knows whether a story is true or not, the story is called a legend?

This is how you play knight!

Make up your own heraldry symbol

You can recognize a knight by his heraldry symbol. In the castle, you saw the symbol on the shutters, the gate, the flags and the banners. Knights often choose an animal for their heraldry symbol. A bear means that the knight is strong and smart. A bee means he is diligent. Which animal would you pick?

Make your own shield

You will need:
a big piece of cardboard, two cardboard strips, scissors, glue, drawing-materials

This is what you do:

1. Draw the shape of your shield on the cardboard, then cut it out.

2. Put your arm on the shield.
   Mark where your elbow and your palm are.
   Use glue on these spots to fasten the two cardboard bands.
   That way, you can hold your shield.

3. When the glue is dry you can paint your heraldry symbol on the front. Your shield is ready!

These knights are really neat

Mini-quiz

1. Where does the word knight come from?

2. Where do knights live?

3. Why do knights live there?

4. What is a shield-bearer?

5. Why do knights wear suits of armor?

6. Are knights the only ones to wear armor?

7. What is a heraldry symbol?

8. What does a jester do?

9. Name some famous knights.

10. What is a legend?